—Oceans

© Aladdin Books Ltd

Designed and produced by
Aladdin Books Ltd
70 Old Compton Street
London W1

Published in the USA in 1984 by
Franklin Watts
387 Park Avenue South
New York, NY 10016

Library of Congress
Catalog Card No 84-51227

ISBN 0-531-04835-7

Printed in Belgium

FRANKLIN WATTS PICTURE ATLAS

Oceans

Martin Bramwell

FRANKLIN WATTS
New York · London · Toronto · Sydney

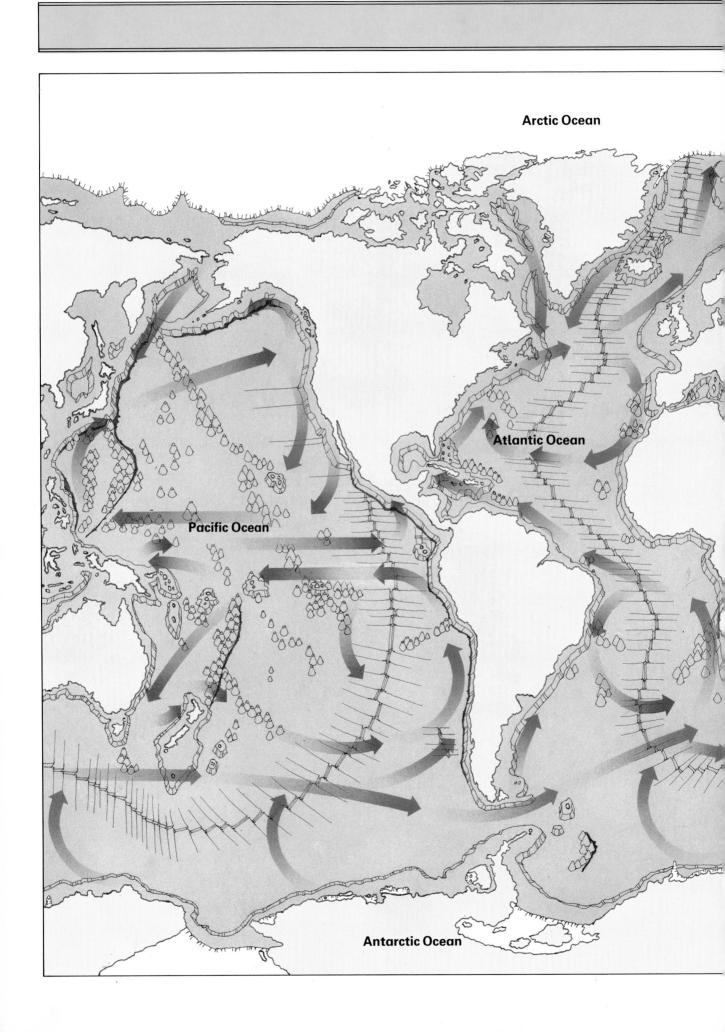

Arctic Ocean

Atlantic Ocean

Pacific Ocean

Antarctic Ocean

Foreword

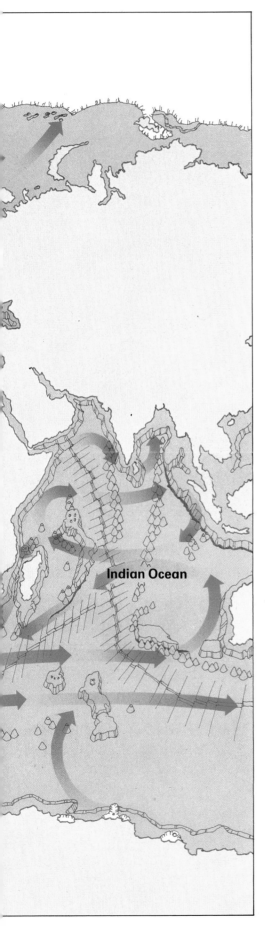

Indian Ocean

The oceans have fascinated mankind for thousands of years – probably ever since people stood on a seashore wondering where the waves came from and what lay beyond the far horizon. But in those distant days the sea was also something to be feared. It was the home of storm gods, monsters and unknown dangers. Many centuries were to pass before men ventured out of sight of land.

The sea still fascinates us, even though many of its mysteries have now been solved. Today we fly across the greatest ocean without a second thought. Cargo ships of every shape and size cross the seas carrying food, fuel, raw materials and factory goods. Modern fishing boats use high technology to hunt the shoals of fish, then process and freeze the catch on board. But in many parts of the world men still fish the seas in traditional ways, using nets and lines from sailing boats and outrigger canoes.

For ocean scientists the past 30 years have produced a flood of new and exciting information. Like a good detective story, the clues slowly came together – from seabed rocks and from fossils on land, from modern volcanoes, and from traces of magnetism in ancient rocks. And out of it all came a picture of the colossal geological forces that have changed the face of the Earth in ages past – and that are still changing it today.

Contents

The Undersea Landscape

Imagine a landscape with mountains greater than the Himalayas, plains that would dwarf those of Africa and Asia, and trenches that would swallow up the Grand Canyon. Such a landscape exists – at the bottom of the world's oceans – and it has been built by enormous forces that have torn the earth's rocky skin into pieces and shuffled those pieces around time and time again over millions of years.

The idea that the continents have moved is not new. It was first suggested over 130 years ago. But then it seemed too far-fetched and ridiculous to be true, and the idea was ignored. As the years passed, more evidence built up until the invention of echo sounders and equipment for sampling and studying the seabed, paved the way for a breakthrough in the 1960s.

We now know that the earth's crust is made up of eight very large pieces, and a number of smaller ones, and that these pieces, called "plates" by geologists, are being dragged over the surface of the earth by movements in a semi-molten rock layer below the stony crust.

Ridges, trenches and islands

The mountainous ridges that run for 40,000 km (25,000 miles) across the ocean basins are formed where new rock is being forced to the surface. Once there, it is carried away at either side of the ridge by the "conveyor-belt action" of the plates. But the earth is not getting any bigger, so where does the extra rock go? The answer lies in the deep trenches at the edges of the oceans. Here, the ocean plate is forced down beneath the continental plate. The grinding of the moving plates and the melting of the seabed rocks as they are pulled deep into the earth are the cause of earthquakes and volcanic eruptions. The power of these forces is hard to imagine. When India drifted north, and crashed into Asia 35 million years ago its seabed rocks were thrust 8 km (5 miles) into the sky – forming today's Himalayas.

The conveyor-belt action of the ocean floor is also proved by the islands of the Pacific. Most of them were formed by volcanic eruptions over "hot spots" in the crust. The islands were then carried on, and gradually worn away.

Sea level   **Mid-ocean ridge**   **Trench**

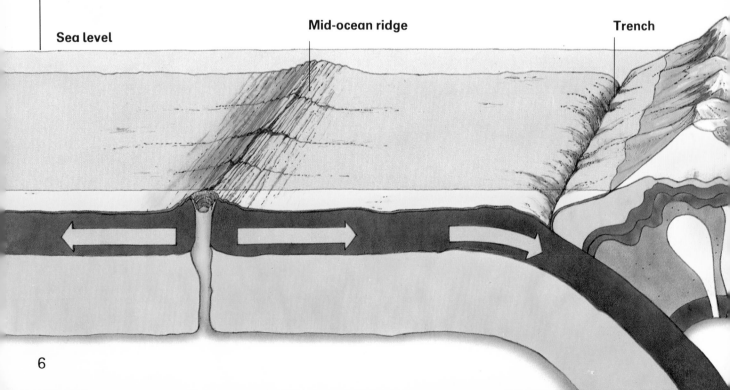

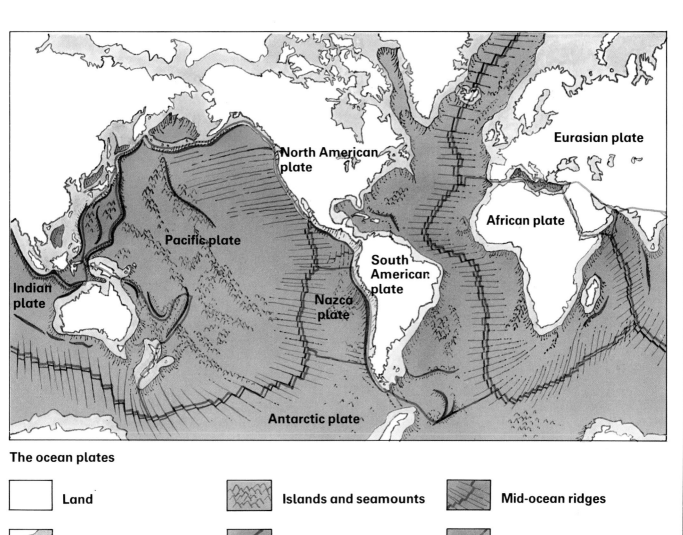

The ocean plates

| | Land | | Islands and seamounts | | Mid-ocean ridges |
| | Continental shelf | | Major trenches | | Plate boundaries |

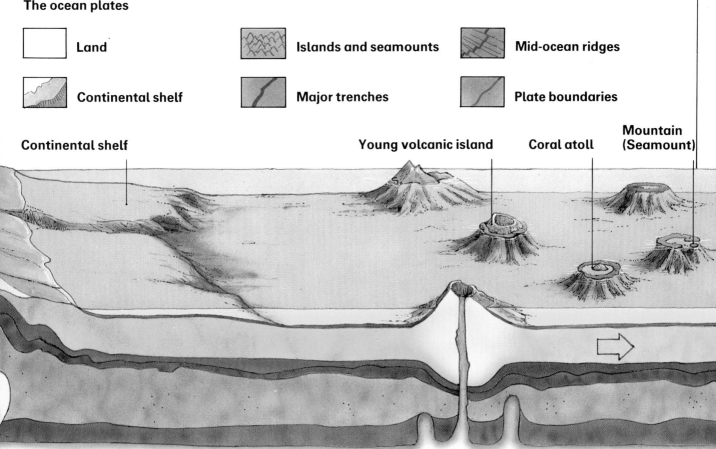

Continental shelf   Young volcanic island   Coral atoll   Mountain (Seamount)

Currents and Tides

The surging tides are powered by forces beyond the earth. The force of gravity pulls the ocean waters into a bulge toward the Moon, and as the Moon travels around the earth, this watery bulge tries to follow it. This causes the water to surge back and forth like water in a bowl. The high spring tides happen when the Sun and Moon are in line, and the Sun's pull reinforces that of the Moon. The much smaller neap tides occur when sun and moon are pulling at right angles.

Ocean currents are powered by the wind. Near the equator, the trade winds push the surface waters toward the west until they meet land. The currents then swing away from the equator and the trade winds push the waters back to the east so that a great circular movement is built up in each of the ocean basins.

Wind rushing over the water surface sets up tiny waves, and these grow bigger and bigger the longer the wind keeps blowing. The wind pushes against the upwind side of the wave, while eddies form at the downwind side. These lower the pressure there, and also help the wave along as shown below.

The tides

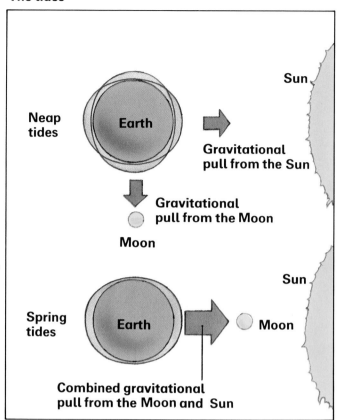

Neap tides

Earth

Sun

Gravitational pull from the Sun

Gravitational pull from the Moon

Moon

Spring tides

Earth

Sun

Moon

Combined gravitational pull from the Moon and Sun

"Tidal waves" (*tsunamis*) are caused by submarine earthquakes. At sea they are usually 1 m (3 ft) high, but they can travel at up to 800 kph (500 mph). When they hit shallow coastal waters they can rear up to 40 m (130 ft) high.

Winds and currents

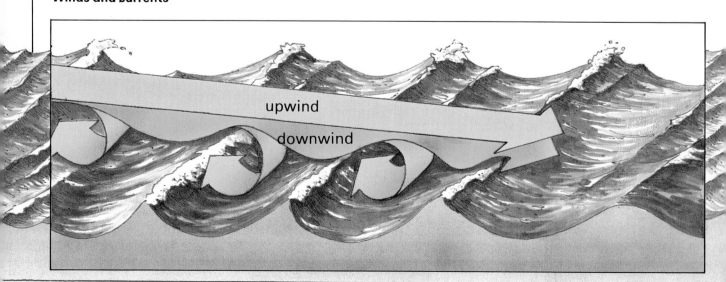

upwind

downwind

Warm and cold currents of the world's oceans

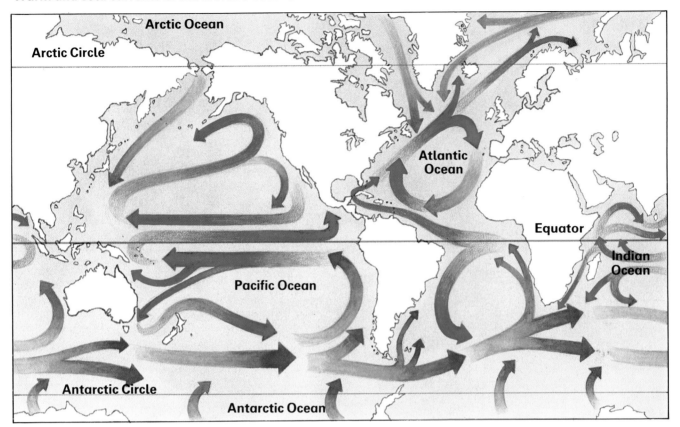

Part of the enjoyment of the coast lies in the marvelous variety of its scenery. It is carved by the sea, with help by wind, rain and frost, and the type of scenery in any particular place depends on how sheltered it is, and what sort of rock it is made of.

The constant pounding of the waves on land may produce steep cliffs, dramatic arches and offshore stacks. On sheltered shores the sea may build and produce sandy beaches and dunes, or narrow bars and banks of sand and pebbles.

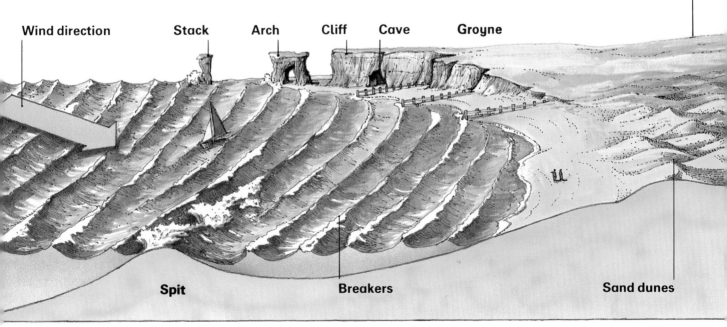

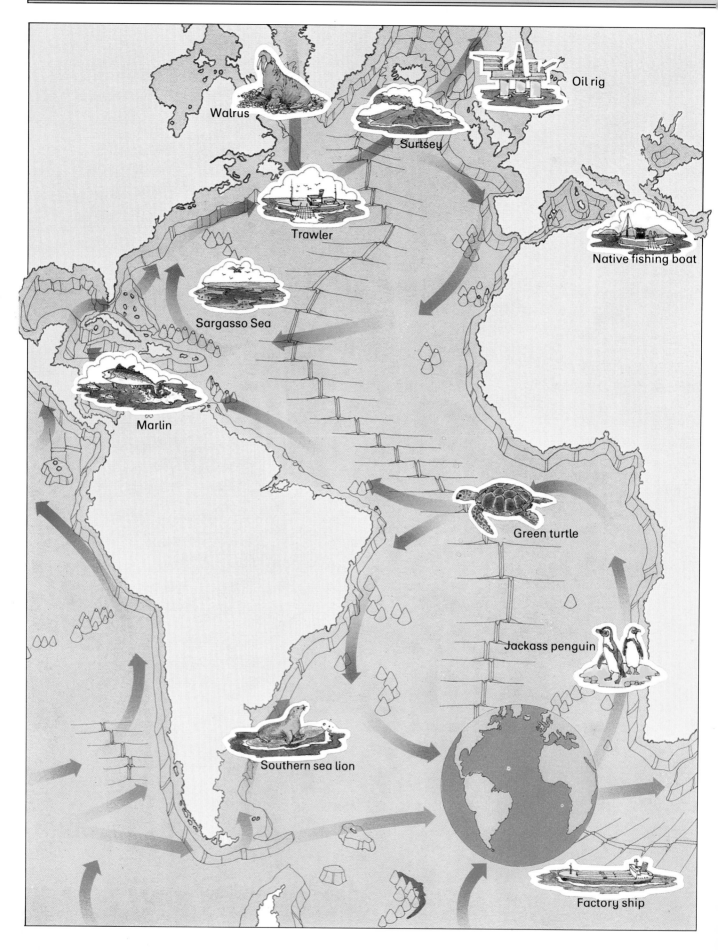

Walrus

Surtsey

Oil rig

Trawler

Native fishing boat

Sargasso Sea

Marlin

Green turtle

Jackass penguin

Southern sea lion

Factory ship

Atlantic Ocean

The most spectacular feature of the Atlantic Ocean floor is the huge mountain ridge running down its center from the edge of the Arctic Ocean to far beyond the tip of South Africa. For most of its length, the ridge top lies more than 1.6 km (1 mile) beneath the ocean surface, but in a few places – such as Iceland in the north and the Ascension islands (Ponape) just south of the equator – it breaks the surface to form volcanic islands. The newest of these is Surtsey, born in 1963 when a violent eruption on the underwater ridge south of Iceland forced masses of molten rock (called lava) to the surface, and sent clouds of volcanic ash and steam high into the atmosphere.

All along the ridge, lava is welling up and adding to the earth's crust, and as these new rocks move slowly apart, the Americas are carried farther to the west, Europe and Africa are carried farther to the east, and the Atlantic Ocean gets wider by about 4 cm (1.5 in) a year.

In the ocean depths at either side of the ridge, the seabed rocks are covered by fine mud, usually less than 0.8 km (0.5 miles) thick. But at the edges of the oceans, where rivers wash huge amounts of sand, silt and mud from the land, the rocks of the seabed may be buried more than 4.8 km (3 miles) deep. Off parts of North America and Africa these great thicknesses of sediment have been building up ever since the Atlantic Ocean started as a crack between North America and Europe, 200 million years ago.

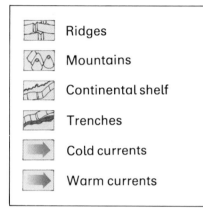

	Ridges
	Mountains
	Continental shelf
	Trenches
	Cold currents
	Warm currents

The Atlantic coast off Portugal

Wildlife

Far out in the middle of a big ocean it would be easy to think that the seas hold very little life. But this is because everything is spread over such an enormous area, and most of it is out of sight anyway. Close to land it is a different story. Along the shoreline there are creatures of all kinds crawling over the rocks, burrowing into the sand and swimming beneath the waves.

Smallest of all sea life are the tiny plants that drift near the surface. Like the grasses and trees on land, they use the sun's energy to make new plants. Minute animals feed on these plants, and together they are called plankton. They are the main food for everything else that lives in the sea. Other creatures either eat plankton – or other animals that are plankton feeders. Two of the oceans' biggest animals live entirely on plankton. They are the 30 m (100 ft) blue whale and the 18 m (60 ft) basking shark.

Crowded cliffs and lonely wanderers

Birds are the most noticeable wildlife along the North Atlantic coasts. Terns and plovers, gulls and oystercatchers are a common sight on sandy and muddy shores, but most spectacular of all are the huge colonies of guillemot, gannets, kittiwakes and razorbills that live on steep sea cliffs in the far north. The island of St Kilda off the Scottish coast is home to more than 100,000 gannets. The South Atlantic has none of these huge colonies but this vast expanse of ocean is home to the great wandering albatross. These seas are also home to storm petrels, Antarctic terns, and several kinds of penguin, including the rockhopper and jackass.

Guillemot colony in Scandinavia

Green turtle

The long-distance travelers

The oceans are home to some of nature's truly long-range travelers. Migration is common in many sea creatures. Among the birds, for example, the Arctic tern breeds in the Arctic tundra but migrates as far south as Antarctica. Many species of fish, too, make complicated annual journeys, often in the form of a roughly circular loop from the spawning grounds where the young are born, to nursery areas, and then finally to the main feeding grounds. These migrations usually take place within the huge swirling patterns of the ocean currents. The timing of the migrations is also vitally important. If the young fish are to survive, they must be born when plankton food is plentiful.

European eels are also amazing travelers. They are spawned in the warm waters of the Sargasso Sea, and currents carry the larvae across the Atlantic where they swim into the rivers of Europe as young eels (elvers.) They remain there until they are fully grown, then make the long journey back to the Sargasso Sea.

But birds and fish are not the only animals that perform feats of navigation. The Atlantic green turtle feeds on the shores of Brazil, but it seems they swim 2250 km (1400 miles), against the current, to reach their breeding grounds on the beaches of Ascension Island (Ponape) in the middle of the Atlantic Ocean.

Jackass penguins, South Atlantic

Tuna fishing off the Libyan coast

13

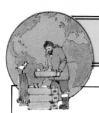
Europeans have been using the sea for many thousands of years. Their earliest boats were probably rafts and dugout canoes, and wood-framed skin boats like coracles and kayaks. But before long, much more seaworthy craft were made and sea trading began. We know, for example, that more than 5,000 years ago people living around the shores of the Mediterranean Sea used ships for trading.

The real revolution in sea travel, however, came about 500 years ago, when several new methods of navigation were invented. Bigger and better ships were developed, and the great age of exploration began. European seafarers and adventurers set their ships' courses to the west and south in search of new lands.

During the following 200 years, the world's oceans became the highways for a worldwide network of trade routes. Spices were carried from the islands of Southeast Asia, cotton and tea from India, and gold and ivory from Africa.

Times change, and today the main cargoes are crude oil, metals, chemicals, lumber and other raw materials; food such as wheat, dairy products and frozen meat; and manufactured goods of every kind. The Atlantic is still the main highway. More than half the world's tanker and cargo trade moves in and out of the ports of Western Europe.

Food for the cities

Small-scale coastal fishing has always been an important way of life around the shores of the Atlantic. But more than 400 years ago the fishermen of Britain, Scandinavia and Holland were already

Fishing for cod, North Atlantic

sailing far out into the North Sea, and beyond into the wild waters of Iceland and Norway, in search of the great shoals of silver herring. Later, boats crossed the Atlantic to fish the rich stocks of cod off the coast of Newfoundland, while boats from many nations also hunted seals and whales for their valuable oil and skins.

As the cities of Europe and America grew, so did the demand for food. Bigger boats and better nets were developed, and today fishing in the Atlantic is mainly carried out by large factory ships using echo sounders to find the shoals and special machinery to clean and freeze the fish ready for market. Herring and sardines are caught with circular purse seine nets. Fish living nearer the bottom, like cod, and flounder, are fished with huge bag-shaped trawl nets.

New wealth from the seas

More than a quarter of the world's oil now comes from beneath the sea. The North Sea is the newest of the Atlantic's oil-producing regions, but others are found off the coasts of Nigeria, South Africa, Brazil and southern Argentina, in addition to the big oilfields of the Gulf of Mexico, and Lake Maracaibo in Venezuela.

Oil is the most valuable mineral product of the Atlantic, but there are others. Sand and gravel are dredged for building material, and a special calcium sand used for cement, glass making and other processes is taken from the shallow seas of the Bahamas in the biggest ocean mining operation in the world. In the future, many minerals, including tin and gold, may be taken from the Atlantic's continental shelf areas.

Drilling for oil, North Atlantic

The busy oil port of Lagos, Nigeria

Mexican shrimping boat

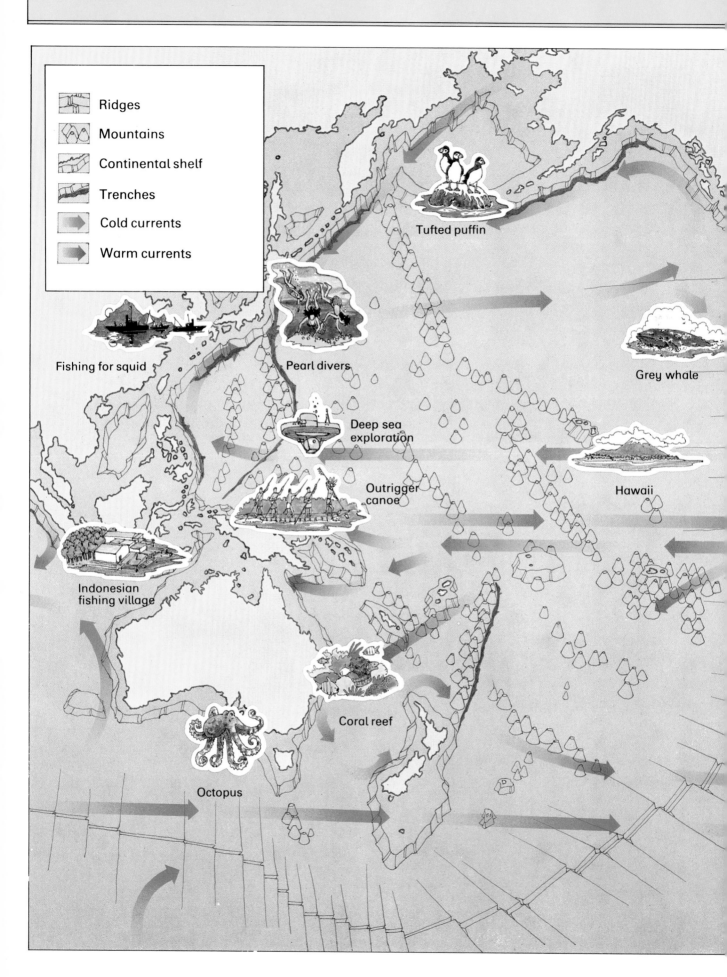

Ridges

Mountains

Continental shelf

Trenches

Cold currents

Warm currents

Tufted puffin

Fishing for squid

Pearl divers

Grey whale

Deep sea exploration

Outrigger canoe

Hawaii

Indonesian fishing village

Octopus

Coral reef

Pacific Ocean

The Pacific Ocean is by far the largest of the world's oceans. It covers roughly one-third of the earth's surface, and is so big that viewed from a certain angle in space it seems to cover one face of the earth completely. But despite its great size, the Pacific is the one ocean that has been shrinking for millions of years. It is what is left of the great ocean that surrounded the primitive "supercontinent" before Antarctica, Africa, the Americas, India and Asia split up. The Pacific still has a very active ridge – spreading as fast as 17 cm (6.5 in) a year in places – but all around its shores are the deep trenches and arcs of volcanic islands that show where the seabed is being dragged deep into the earth and destroyed. There are more earthquakes and volcanic eruptions here than anywhere else on earth, and geologists have called this the "Pacific Ring of Fire."

The seabed in the eastern part of the Pacific is quite young; in the west it is much older; instead of being fairly flat it is studded with thousands of islands, some quite large and new, others so old that their tops have long sunk beneath the waves. They were formed in long lines or chains as the ocean crust moved slowly, like a conveyor belt, over volcanic "hot spots."

Marine iguana

Cormorant

Coral islands in the Pacific

The coral reefs of the Pacific are among the most colorful of all marine habitats, and none are more spectacular than the Great Barrier Reef that runs for more than 1900 km (1200 miles) along the eastern Australian coast. The hard rock of the reef is made up of the skeletons of millions of tiny sea creatures called coral polyps. The skeletons are usually white, but the flesh of the living polyps which grow upon them may be brilliant red, orange, purple, yellow or green, so the living reef is a kaleidoscope of color. But not all the reef residents are colorful. The deadly stonefish, one of the most dangerous of the poisonous fishes, lies motionless on the seabed looking just like dead coral.

The reef is full of specialists, too. Some fish have very deep bodies, flattened so that they can slip easily between the branching corals. Some are immune to the paralyzing stings of anemones and jellyfish, and even live among their tentacles, safe from other hunters. There are parrot fish with powerful jaws designed for crunching the living coral, and busy cleaner fish that hover near other fish, picking up food and cleaning parasites from their skin.

But coral reefs are fragile as well as beautiful. The tiny polyps are easily killed if their waters are polluted. They have natural enemies too. In recent years great damage has been done to Pacific and Indian Ocean reefs by the bizarre and rather sinister-looking "crown of thorns" — a large starfish that actually feeds on the coral.

Brown pelicans in the Pacific

Marine iguanas and Land crabs, Galápagos Islands

Mammals of the Pacific

At the opposite side of the ocean from the Great Barrier Reef, the remarkable sea otter makes its home among the waving beds of giant kelp seaweed off the coasts of Alaska and California. This curious animal spends all its time in the sea, and even sleeps lying on its back on the surface. It feeds on shellfish which it catches by diving to the seabed. Born on land, the pups soon enter the water, often sleeping on their mother's chest as she floats. Another marvel of the California coast is the 17 m (50 ft) grey whale that returns every year to breed in the shallow lagoons of the Gulf of California.

Island refuge or island prison?

The islands of the Pacific hold some of the world's most rare and interesting creatures. The Galapagos Islands in the eastern Pacific are home to the Galápagos penguin, the strange flightless cormorant, prehistoric-looking iguanas that live on land but feed in the sea, and bright red land crabs. The giant tortoises and unusual finches of the islands started the great naturalist Charles Darwin thinking about his theory of evolution when he visited the Galapagos Islands in 1835.

But while some islands are protected havens of peace for wildlife, others have been wrecked by humans. Many of the islands off the coast of Chile, used by countless boobies and cormorants, have been almost totally destroyed by mining companies digging out the guano (bird droppings) for use as phosphate fertilizer.

Humpback whale, Alaska

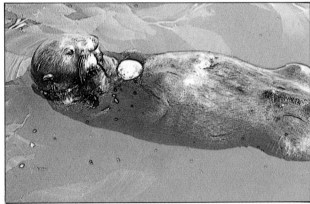

Sea otter feeding on shellfish

People

The vast Pacific Ocean saw some of the world's first great sea voyages. Australia and New Guinea were settled by people from Asia more than 30,000 years ago, and that would have been impossible without sturdy craft of some kind. More recently, between 5000 and 2000 years ago, Asian settlers spread out to nearly every one of the scattered islands of the Pacific, probably using large outrigger canoes similar to those still used today in many traditional ceremonies. All too easily we think of Europeans such as Columbus and Magellan as the great voyagers and navigators. In many ways

they were, but we should also remember that Easter Island, one of the most remote of the Pacific islands, was settled by people sailing open boats, with no scientific navigation instruments. And by the seventh century AD Chinese traders were sailing their junks to Indonesia, and on across the Indian Ocean to Africa.

The Indonesian archipelago contains more than 13,000 islands, so it is hardly surprising that many of its people have a seafaring history. As well as traveling north to China, Indonesian traders crossed to India and the coast of Africa more than 2000 years ago.

Surfing on Pacific breakers, Hawaii

Modern junks in Hong Kong harbor

The world's greatest fishery

Of all the fish taken from the sea each year nearly half are taken from the Pacific.

Fishing has been a traditional way of life for many people living around the Pacific. The Eskimos fished with spears and lines. The Indonesian islanders still use nets and fish traps. Pacific islanders also use nets and lines from their outrigger canoes, and laid nets out to sea from the beaches.

Modern fisheries also use many methods. The huge catches of anchovies taken off the coast of Peru and Chile are caught by small boats using purse seine nets. Cod, flounder, sea bass and other bottom-dwellers are caught by large trawlers, especially in the Arctic, in the seas around Japan, and in the South China Sea. The big Pacific tuna are hunted in powerful boats, far out in mid-ocean.

There are specialized fishing grounds too. Shark fishing is important off the Australian coast. King crabs are caught with tangling nets and other traps off the shores of Alaska. Pearl divers work the shallow coastal waters off Japan, while farther out to sea, Japanese fishermen with many-hooked "jigging lines" use lights to lure squid near their boats at night.

Fishing from out rigger canoes, the Society Islands

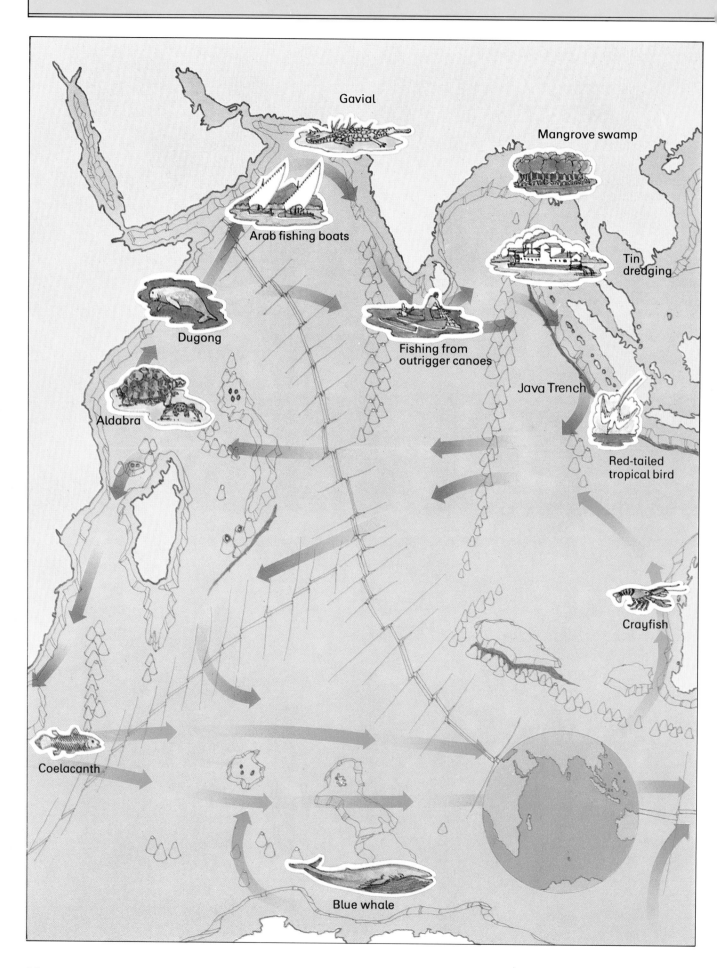

Gavial

Mangrove swamp

Arab fishing boats

Tin dredging

Dugong

Fishing from outrigger canoes

Aldabra

Java Trench

Red-tailed tropical bird

Crayfish

Coelacanth

Blue whale

Indian Ocean

The seabed of the Indian Ocean is a complicated pattern of ridges and trenches, shallow seas and deep ocean basins, and the reason for this lies in its history. About 140 million years ago Africa, Antarctica, Australia and India were all joined together. Then Africa and Antarctica split apart along the line of the Southwest Indian Ridge. About 20 million years after that, a second split opened up and India started to drift north, leaving Antarctica and Australia behind. Finally, about 36 million years ago, Australia and Antarctica were carried apart at either side of the main Mid Indian Ocean Ridge. The most interesting part of the ridge system today is the side branch that runs into the Red Sea. For the past 25 million years this ridge has been carrying Africa and Arabia farther and farther apart.

The only deep trench in the Indian Ocean is the 7440 m (24,400 ft) Java Trench. It marks the line where the Indian Ocean floor is being dragged into the earth's crust beneath the islands of Southeast Asia. Although scientists think it is a very young trench, it has already provided some of the biggest volcanic eruptions the world has ever seen. In 1883, explosions blew the island of Krakatoa apart. Huge tidal waves swept round the shores of the Indian Ocean, doing enormous damage, and the biggest explosion of all was heard 4800 km (3000 miles) away in Australia.

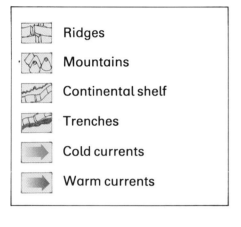

Ridges

Mountains

Continental shelf

Trenches

Cold currents

Warm currents

Mangrove swamps found around the shores of the Indian Ocean

In 1938, in the southern part of the Indian Ocean, a discovery was made that amazed ocean scientists. Local fishermen off the coast of South Africa hauled in their nets and found they had caught a large primitive-looking fish nearly 1.5 m (5 ft) long and weighing more than 54 kg (120 pounds). The fish had big heavy fins and powerful jaws, and probably lived by hunting other deep-water animals living in the seabed mud. What surprised experts was that the fish was a coelacanth – a species that they thought had been extinct for more than 60 million years, and was previously known only from fossil remains.

The world's threatened islands

We all have a romantic picture of what coral islands are like, but these tiny scraps of land far out in the oceans have often been very badly treated by humans. The problem for island birds is that as soon as people arrive they start hunting. The crews of sailing ships hunted mainly for food, but unfortunately cats and rats also got ashore from the ships, and the local wildlife stood little chance against these expert hunters. In modern times, birds with beautiful feathers have been shot in their millions for the fashion trade, and islands have been ruined in the search for

Robber crab on Aldabra Island

Olive sea snake

Damsel fish and coral, Red Sea,

minerals, or have had their forests cut down to provide land for farming.

Fortunately, some islands are now cared for as wildlife reserves. The Indian Ocean island of Aldabra, for example, was threatened with the building of a military airfield until conservationists managed to get the plans scrapped. It was a narrow escape. Aldabra is home to thousands of giant tortoises, huge robber crabs, many plant species found nowhere else on earth, and a remarkable collection of birds that includes some of the world's rarest species. Very few visitors, other than scientists, are allowed onto the island.

Flying fish and swimming snakes
The warm waters of the Indian Ocean are home to many interesting animals. Flying fish skip over the surface as they try to escape from fast-swimming hunting fish like marlin and tuna, while slow, harmless dugongs feed on water plants in the shallow coastal waters, safe from the sharks and killer whales that patrol the deeper waters. Mangrove swamps are home to sea snakes and crab-eating frogs, tree-climbing crabs and gavials, a type of crocodile, and strangest of all, the tropical mudskippers – primitive fish that scurry over the surface of the mud.

People

The northern part of the Indian Ocean differs from the other great oceans in one important way. Its current system changes direction twice each year. In the summer, when the south west monsoons are blowing, the currents move in a clockwise direction like those of the Atlantic and Pacific. The warm winds become saturated with water as they blow across the Bay of Bengal, and it is these winds that bring the daily rains and frequent flooding that is typical of the low-lying parts of Southeast Asia. In winter, the currents change and swirl in the opposite direction, driven by the strong north east monsoon winds that blow from the heartlands of Asia.

The southern Indian Ocean behaves in a more normal manner. The very fast Agulhas Current sweeps down the coast of South Africa at more than 160 km (100 miles) a day, then flows east toward Australia before turning north again to complete the loop. The waters off the South African coast are often very dangerous. Here, the fast-flowing Agulhas Current meets the big waves surging north from storms in the Antarctic region. Where the two meet, giant waves are formed, and many ships have been completely overwhelmed by them. Despite this, the Indian Ocean has been a major highway for thousands of years. Chinese traders reached the African coast in their junks long before European seafarers arrived, and earlier still, perhaps 2500 years ago,

Oil tanker in the Persian Gulf

traders from the Indonesian islands crossed the Indian Ocean on the west-flowing currents. They left their mark too, for the language of Madagascar is quite unlike the nearby African languages.

Resources of the ocean

The Indian Ocean has a very small continental shelf area, and this is one reason why its fisheries have never become as important as those of other oceans. Most of the fishing is traditional. The only commercial fisheries are those for sailfish, tuna and marlin carried out in deep waters by boats from Japan and Korea. In recent years shrimp fishing has become an important industry off Arabia, Pakistan and India, while Australian cray fishermen take a rich harvest, most of which is exported to the United States.

The coral reefs of the Red Sea and the East African coast provide another source of trade, but the corals and shells are often harvested without any care for the reef, and terrible damage is being done.

The main mineral wealth of the area is, of course, the oil in the Persian Gulf. This one small area provides more than a third of the world's oil. But oil and gas exploration is under way all around the shores of the Indian Ocean, and in the past few years large oilfields have been found off Western Australia. And the narrow continental shelves of the Indian Ocean are rich in tin and a variety of other minerals that can be dredged from the seabed.

Shallow water fishing in Sri Lanka

The fish market in Dhubai, Persian Gulf

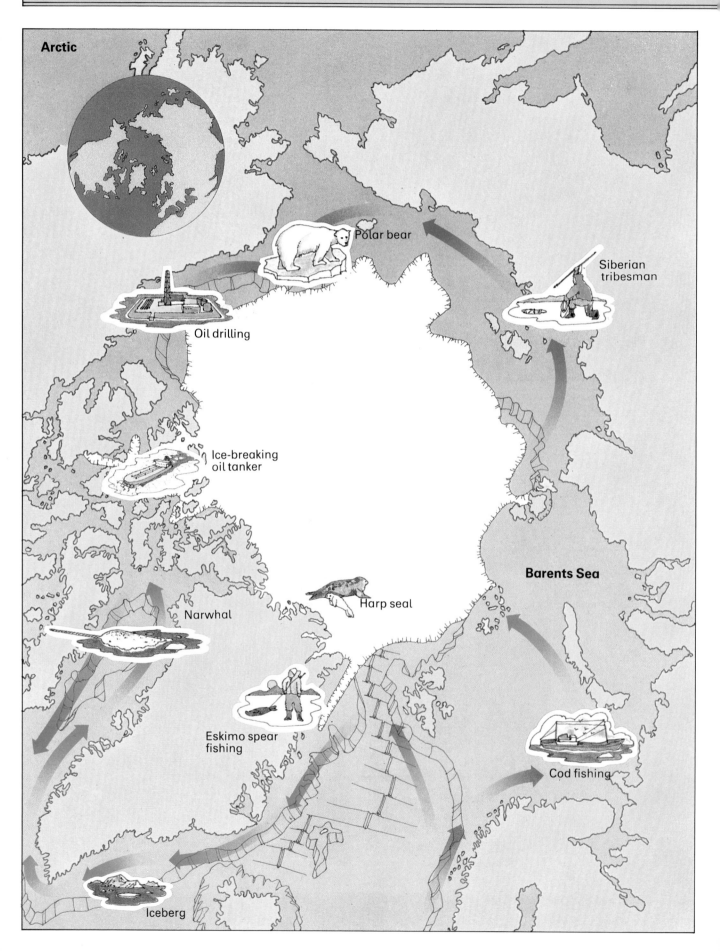

Arctic

Polar bear

Siberian tribesman

Oil drilling

Ice-breaking oil tanker

Barents Sea

Harp seal

Narwhal

Eskimo spear fishing

Cod fishing

Iceberg

Arctic and Antarctic Oceans

The two great polar regions have just one thing in common. They are both cold, ice-covered wildernesses. But in nearly every other way they are very, very different. The Arctic is an ocean, almost completely surrounded by land and covered by ice throughout the year. The pack ice is constantly on the move, sometimes cracking to give patches of open water, then piling into great jagged heaps as the polar winds drive it along. One of the Arctic Ocean's most important features is its huge area of continental shelf. Along the Canadian side the shelf is the usual width of 80 to 240 km (50 to 150 miles) but off the northern coast of Asia it is anything up to 1200 km (750 miles) wide. Because so many fish species like shallow shelf areas, the Barents Sea in particular is one of the world's richest fishing grounds. And as the world demands more and more oil, the shelf areas of the Arctic look more and more promising to oilmen – despite the bitter cold, the howling winds and the 24-hour darkness of the winter months.

By contrast, Antarctica's continental shelf is very narrow, and the continental slope plunges steeply into ocean basins more than 4600 m (15,000 ft) deep. In winter nearly 20.7 million sq km (8 million sq miles) of the Antarctic Ocean are completely frozen, but in summer much of the ice melts, breaks up, and drifts out into the southern oceans.

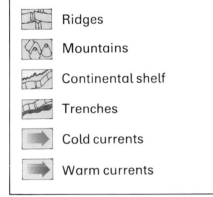

Ridges

Mountains

Continental shelf

Trenches

Cold currents

Warm currents

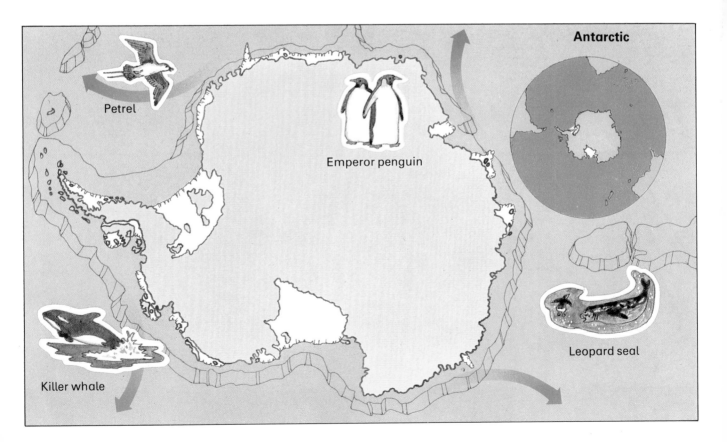

Petrel

Emperor penguin

Killer whale

Leopard seal

Antarctic

People

The Eskimo people of Greenland, Canada and Alaska used to live entirely by hunting and fishing. Walruses and seals were speared through holes in the ice when they came up to breathe, or they were hunted with hand-thrown harpoons from light skin-covered boats called kayaks. Fishing lines were lowered through holes cut in the sea ice, and fish were also caught with nets and spears in the great northern rivers. The Arctic people of Europe and Asia followed a similar way of life, but those areas also had a long tradition of reindeer herding.

In the past, these people were nearly all nomadic, living in snow houses and skin tents. When European traders arrived in the north, the Eskimos traded furs and seal skins for guns, and for modern boats with motors. Recent years have seen even bigger changes. Snowmobiles have almost replaced sleds and dog-teams. Most of the Eskimos now live in villages built with government help, and many work in factories freezing or canning fish.

Eskimos in west Greenland

Wildlife

The very cold ice-covered waters in the middle of the Arctic Ocean are not very rich in animal life, but around the edges it is a very different story. Here the Arctic waters mix with the warmer waters of the North Atlantic and North Pacific oceans, and the sea life is much more varied and plentiful. In the Arctic summer the sun rides high in the sky all day, and its life-giving rays go deep into the water to help the growth of the plankton "harvest." Rivers flowing from the surrounding continents add to the food supply by carrying nutrients far out into the continental shelf seas. Squid, seals, baleen whales and shoals of fish feed on

Polar bear

the masses of plankton, and they in turn provide food for the killer whales, who can sprint at more than 72 kph (45 mph) when hunting.

On the surface, flocks of seabirds wheel and dive and swim after their prey, while the huge polar bear stalks across the ice looking for unwary seals. Many stories are told of the hunting skills of the polar bear, and one says that when closing in for the kill, he holds one paw over his shiny black nose in case the dark spot gives him away against the glistening white snow.

In deeper waters, walruses swim down to the seabed and use their long tusks to dig clams and other shellfish from the mud. And in the deepest waters of all, lives the ugly wolf fish, another clam-crusher with huge powerful jaws, and the cod and haddock that feed on small fish, sea urchins, sand worms and starfish on the ocean floor.

Abuse of the Arctic

While the Eskimos took from the Arctic only what they needed, things have changed. Today, large-scale hunting poses a real threat to the balance of nature. Every year, for instance, thousands of young harp seals are killed for their beautiful silver-white fur.

Harp seal pup

Puffin

Mention Antarctica and most people think of penguins. There are 16 different species, and most live among the scattered islands of the southern oceans and along the southern shores of South America, South Africa, Australia and New Zealand. But five are truly Antarctic, and four of these spend most of the year at sea among the pack ice, only coming ashore to breed in the Antarctic spring. The fifth is the magnificent 115 cm (42 in) tall Emperor penguin, whose long breeding season includes the bitter Antarctic winter. The female lays her egg and then goes off to sea to feed, leaving the male to care for the egg – in a most unusual way. He rests the egg on top of his feet and covers it with a warm flap of skin on his belly. He can even shuffle about without dropping it. The temperature may be −50°C (−58°F) or colder, but the egg stays at a cozy +33°C (+91°F) until it hatches in the spring, just when food is most plentiful.

Penguins are a marvelous piece of design work by nature. They have a dense covering of short springy feathers and a thick layer of blubber under the skin, and these protect them from the cold.

Sharing the ocean food store

The different seals of the Antarctic waters share the habitat without competing for food. The big Weddell seals stay close to land and feed on fish. The common crabeater seals live out among the pack ice and feed on krill and squid. And the fierce leopard seal patrols the edges of the pack ice, hunting for weak or isolated penguins.

Farther north, in the slightly warmer waters of the southern oceans, huge

Krill

Crabeater seals on sea ice

elephant seals and fur seals breed on the rocky shores of the scattered islands. Bull elephant seals can grow to 6 m (19 ft) long and weigh more than 4.06 tonnes (4 tons). During the breeding season, each of the huge old "beachmasters" defends his own stretch of beach, and his collection of "wives," and fierce battles often break out between the old males and the younger bulls who are trying to claim beach territories of their own.

In the days of the sealers, millions of fur seals were killed among these same islands, partly for their valuable furs and partly for the oil that could be made from their blubber. Fortunately that is one kind of hunting that has now ended. Far too many seals were being killed, and many colonies almost disappeared. Now these beautiful wild animals are left in peace and their numbers are increasing again.

One very big difference between the Arctic region and Antarctica is that the great southern continent has no native people. The only humans there are visitors, and in order to survive there they must take with them everything they need – food, buildings, fuel and transportation.

The first visitors to the edges of the Antarctic were the sealers and whalers who discovered there were sheltered natural harbors on islands like South Georgia in the South Atlantic. These men mapped parts of Antarctica's coastline. Later, men set out to explore Antarctica, and many heroic journeys were made before the great Norwegian explorer Roald Amundsen reached the South Pole on December 14, 1911.

Today, Antarctica is a place for scientists. It is the best place on earth for studying the higher levels of the atmosphere, and all the research bases have weather stations. Geologists and glaciologists use aircraft and motorized sleds to explore the land and the 3.2 km (2 mile) thick ice, while biologists make detailed studies of the rich sea life of the Antarctic Ocean.

Research station in Antarctica

The Future of the Environment

Until quite recently many people seemed to think that the oceans held a magic key to the future. They thought the seas would feed us, provide power for our homes and factories, and supply many of the minerals that were running short on land. Now we know that it just isn't so. The oceans do have a lot to offer mankind – but they also need very careful looking after in return.

Protecting the fisheries

Most of the world's best fishing grounds are already being fished, and some of them are being fished far too heavily. The best way of getting more food from the sea is by improving our fishing methods – from the fishes' point of view as well as our own. That means taking better care of the fishing grounds, for example by using light nets that do not damage the seabed,

and by not spoiling the fishes' natural food supply or the cleanness of their water. We must also learn not to take out too many fish too quickly, or we will end up with none at all.

Technology and the future

The sediments that collect on the continental shelves often contain iron, tin, diamonds, gold, titanium and other minerals in what geologists call "placer deposits." These minerals have been washed from the land by rivers, and have collected in the layers of sand and mud offshore. At the moment, many of these placer deposits would cost more to get at than they are worth, but some day in the future, when supplies on land run low, they will be well worth the effort.

Scientists have also suggested various ways of using the power of the waves,

Disaster – blazing oil pours from a wrecked tanker

tides and currents to generate electricity. Some tidal power stations have been built, but most of the other ideas will need many more years of research and experimenting.

One day, our technology will make at least some of these possibilities come true, but in the meantime there are urgent problems to be tackled.

Fighting pollution

We will never be able to "farm" the world's oceans properly if we continue to pour all our poisonous waste into them. Oil from tanker collisions ruins beaches. Seabirds are killed when tankers illegally wash out their tanks at sea. Even the chemical fertilizers and insecticides we use to make our farmland more productive, end up in the sea. DDT has been used all over the world for more than 40 years, but so much of it has been washed off the land into the sea that it is now found in the bodies of Antarctic penguins, deep ocean fishes and Pacific seabirds. Dangerous chemicals cannot simply be poured into the sea and be forgotten. They always come back somewhere.

Planning ahead

So what can we do? Perhaps the most important answer is that we shoud learn from mistakes that have been made in the past – and proceed very carefully. The oceans can provide us with a lot of the food we need. They hold huge reserves of minerals. And they may one day provide us with a new source of power. But they will not be able to do any of this if we fail to look after them properly.

Result – one of many thousands of victims

The fastest fish in the world is the tropical sailfish. One has been timed at just over 109 kph (68 mph).

A fully grown blue whale, the biggest animal ever to live on earth, weighs as much as 25 adult male African elephants.

The biggest wave officially recorded measured 34 m (112 ft) from trough to crest.

If the Red Sea keeps widening at its present rate, it will be as wide as the Atlantic in another 200 million years.

The biggest mountain in the world is *not* Mt. Everest. It is the peak of Mauna Kea on the island of Hawaii. Measured from the ocean bed, the mountain is 10,203 m (33,476 ft) high although only 4205 m (13,796 ft) stick up above sea level.

European eels travel 7500 km (4660 miles) from the Baltic Sea to the Sargasso Sea in order to spawn.

If a 1 kg (2.2 lb) iron ball was dropped overboard at the deepest part of the Marianas trench in the Pacific Ocean, it would take just over an hour to hit the seabed.

One of the oldest animal species on earth must be the little two-shelled brachiopod *Lingula* that lives in the Indian and Pacific Oceans. It has remained almost unchanged for about 525 million years.

The world's biggest giant clam was found on the Great Barrier Reef off the coast of Australia. It was more than 1 m (3 ft) across and weighed a quarter of a ton.

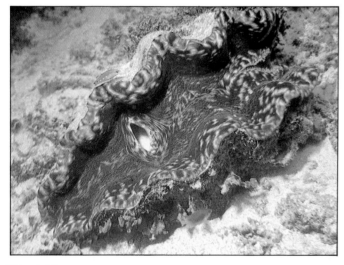

Giant Clam

A huge volcanic eruption that destroyed part of the Mediterranean island of Santorini (now called Thera) in 1400BC probably destroyed the ancient Minoan civilization and started the legend of Atlantis.

Two-shelled molluscs that live on the North Atlantic seabed at 3000 m (10,000 ft) may live for more than 250 years.

Mount Everest started life as part of the ocean floor. When India collided with Asia, the sea that had separated them was crushed, squeezed – and pushed 5 miles into the air. And that is why there are marine fossils high on the world's highest mountain.

The long-distance flying record goes to the Arctic tern. It covers 32,000 km (20,000 miles) every year on its migration from its Arctic breeding grounds to its Antarctic summer quarters.

Sperm whales can dive to depths of 3000 m (10,000 ft) and stay down for nearly two hours.

The huge tabular icebergs that break off the floating ice shelves of Antarctica are often more than 80 km (50 miles) long. The biggest one ever recorded was bigger than Belgium!

The highest tides in the world are at the Bay of Fundy in Nova Scotia, Canada. The incoming tide is funneled into a narrow channel which causes it to rise and fall by 15 m (50 ft).

About five million years ago the Mediterranean Sea dried up. In fact it has dried up and flooded again several times over.

The great Antarctic current that encircles the earth moves at about 19 km (12 miles) a day. Quite slow. But as it reaches down more than 3.2 km (2 miles) it actually moves more than 165 million tons of water every second.

Food is very scarce in the deep ocean basins so some fish, like the gulper eel, have enormous jaws and elastic stomachs so they can swallow fish bigger than themselves.

A 65 ton concrete block used in the breakwater at Cherbourg in France was thrown more than 18 m (60 ft) by a storm wave.

So much water flows into the sea from the Amazon River that the Atlantic is still fresh water almost 160 km (100 miles) from land.

Glossary

Scientists use many special words to describe the geology, water movements and wildlife of the oceans. These are some of the most common ones you are likely to come across.

Abyssal plain The deep ocean floor, usually fairly flat, below 3600 m (12,000 ft).

Annual Something that happens regularly, every year, such as migrations and breeding seasons.

Archipelago A group or chain of islands.

Baleen whales Whales that strain their food from the water by means of sheets of whalebone hanging from the roof of the mouth. (The other main group are the "toothed whales" – killer whales, sperm whales, porpoises and dolphins.)

Bathymetry The study of measuring the depth of the oceans.

Continental shelf The shallow area of seabed around a continent, usually less than 180 m (600 ft) deep. The edge of the shelf marks the true edge of the continent.

Conservationists People who try to persuade others to protect earth's habitats, resources and wildlife, and to use them more wisely.

Crust The outer layer of the earth.

Demersal fish Fish that live on or near the seabed.

Evolution The changes that happen to animals and plants over a period of time.

Gyre The large-scale circulation formed by a group of ocean currents. For example, the Gulf Stream, North Atlantic Current, Canaries Current and North Equatorial Current make up the North Atlantic Gyre.

Habitat The combination of climate, vegetation and animal life that makes up a distinctive set of living conditions. Land habitats include woodland, grassland, marsh and tundra. Marine habitats include salt marshes, coral reefs, deep ocean floors and seaweed beds.

Lagoon A shallow lake or sea, usually surrounded by a reef, with deeper water on the outside.

Larva The early stage in the life of an insect, fish or other sea creature – usually the stage after the egg has hatched.

Lava Molten rock forced out onto the earth's surface from a volcano.

Migration Regular movements of animals. These can be large movements, like the annual journeys made by many birds, fish and other animals, or they can be small movements at regular short intervals. Some plankton, for example, swim up to the surface at night and then swim back to the depths at sunrise so they spend their whole lives in darkness.

Nomadic Having no permanent home. Always on the move.

Nutrients Anything that gives nourishment.

Ooze A very fine seabed mud formed from the remains of marine animals and plants.

Pelagic fish Fish that live in the open seas rather than on the seabed.

Placer deposits Minerals that have been washed off the land by the action of frost, wind, rain and ice, and swept out to sea by rivers. As the mineral grains are heavy, they sink to the seabed and collect in the sea floor mud, often on continental shelves.

Plate tectonics The modern study of the movements of the large raft-like plates that make up the crust of the earth.

Pollution The spoiling of earth's oceans, land habitats, rivers and atmosphere by careless or uncaring dumping of chemicals, gases, garbage and so on.

Prey The animals being hunted. For example, penguins are the main prey of the leopard seal.

Ridge A long range of underwater mountains marking an area where new crust is forming and where two of the earth's crustal plates are moving apart.

Sediment The tiny particles of solid material that slowly sink to the seabed. Most come from the rocks being worn away on land, and these form beds of mud, silt and sand. Others, like some types of limestone, are formed by chemical changes.

Index